Therapy Dogs

BY KARA L. LAUGHLIN

Published in the United States of America by The Child's World®
1980 Lookout Drive • Mankato, MN 56003-1705
800-599-READ • www.childsworld.com

ACKNOWLEDGMENTS
The Child's World®: Mary Berendes, Publishing Director
The Design Lab: Design
Jody Jensen Shaffer: Editing
Pamela J. Mitsakos: Photo Research

PHOTO CREDITS
© Andrew Burgess: leash; remik44992: bone; Denis Kuvaev/
Shutterstock.com: 4-5; iofoto/Shutterstock.com: 16; Ksenia
Raykova/Shutterstock.com: 9; LUGO/iStock.com: 21; Monkey
Business Images/Shutterstock.com: cover, 1, 13; Monkey
Business Images/iStock.com: 14, 19; skynesher/iStock.com: 11;
Tifonimages/Shutterstock.com: 7

ISBN 9781626873131
LCCN 2014934477

Printed in the United States of America
Mankato, MN
July, 2014
PA02219

ABOUT THE AUTHOR

Kara L. Laughlin is the author of eleven books for kids. She lives in Virginia with her husband and three children. They don't have a dog…yet!

TABLE OF CONTENTS

A History of Healing

People with pet dogs know that dogs are hugs in fur clothing. Dogs can calm us down when we are worried. They try to help us when we are hurt. When we are sad, dogs help us feel better. Some dogs take these powers on the road. They share furry friendship with the people who need it most. These dogs are **therapy** dogs.

A man named Dr. Boris Levinson began pet therapy in the 1960s. Dr. Levinson had a dog named Jingles. One day he met with a boy. Jingles was in the office. The boy liked Jingles. He pet Jingles while he talked. Dr. Levinson started to let kids play with his dog. It helped them to talk about hard things. Dr. Levinson wrote about what he did. Others started using dogs for therapy, too.

INTERESTING FACT
The ancient Greeks used dogs to lick wounds clean. They thought that dogs' tongues could heal.

Dogs can help us feel happy, calm, and safe.

A Helping Paw

Today, many places use therapy dogs. Hospitals use them. So do schools and libraries. Most therapy dogs are pets. The owner and the dog work as a team. People pet and talk to the dogs. Sometimes the dogs do tricks. Sometimes people comb them or feed them treats. The dogs help people to feel good.

INTERESTING FACT
Dogs aren't the only ones that can help. Lots of animals are therapy pets. Even alligators!

This therapy dog is letting a little girl put bows in its hair.

7

Crisis Response Dogs

Crisis response dogs are special therapy dogs. They go to places where tragedies have struck. They might go to a school after a fire. They might go to a town after a big storm has hit. These dogs come to people at a very bad time in their lives. Petting a dog can make them feel safer. Sometimes the dogs help people to talk about the things that happened.

INTERESTING FACT
Crisis response dogs also visit rescue workers. The dogs give them a little break. Then they have energy to go back to their jobs.

All kinds of dogs can be crisis response dogs. This is a border collie.

The Science of Therapy Dogs

When we hold a dog, our bodies change. After petting a dog, we feel less stress. We feel loved. Our **blood pressure** goes down. That's good for our hearts. People who are hurt even feel less pain after petting a therapy dog. Therapy dogs really do help people to heal.

INTERESTING FACT
Dr. Sigmund Freud sometimes had his dog, Jo-Fi, in the office. He thought people felt safer with a dog in the office.

Just petting a dog can make people happier and more relaxed.

What Makes a Good Therapy Dog?

A dog of any breed or mix can be a therapy dog. But not every dog can do the job. A therapy dog needs to be good with people and other dogs. He needs to like being petted by strangers. If his owner gives him a command, he must obey. He can't strain at his leash. He needs to be okay in new places. Strange noises and smells can't bother him. He can't bark on visits. He also needs to be clean and well groomed. That's a lot to ask of a dog!

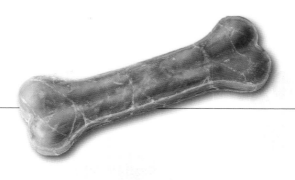

Calm dogs that like people make the best therapy dogs.

13

This therapy dog and its partner are visiting a hospital.

Becoming a Therapy Dog Team

Every therapy dog has a partner. The partner trains the dog to behave well. Then they take a test together. The test is very hard. Testers drop food on the ground. The dogs must leave it alone. They drop heavy books to startle the dogs. The dogs must stay calm. The test can take up to three hours. That's a lot of time for a dog to behave. A dog can't make any mistakes at all. Many dogs do not pass the test.

When a team has passed the test, they go on some visits. A trainer goes along to watch. If she thinks they are ready, the dog gets to be a therapy dog.

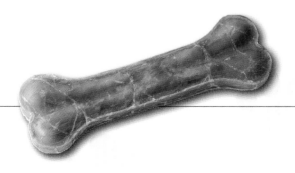

On the Job

Therapy dogs work in many places. Some therapy dogs only do one kind of job. Some do many. The dog's handler gets to choose the job. She picks jobs that she will like. She makes sure the dog will like them, too.

Therapy dogs bring lots of happiness to patients in nursing homes.

Dogs in Hospitals

Some dogs visit people in hospitals. A dog in a hospital is a big treat! Patients get to pet and play with the dogs. Sometimes the dogs get right up in bed with people! Some therapy dogs help injured people to relearn skills. They might fetch balls for a person who is learning to throw.

Dogs with Kids

Some dogs work with children. They might go to a school or a library. A dog might sit while a child reads him stories. It gives the child a chance to practice. (Maybe someday a child will read this book to a therapy dog!)

Dogs with the Elderly

Some dogs visit people in nursing homes. In many nursing homes, people can't have their own pets. They like to see the therapy dogs. They often talk about pets they used to have. Some people say that the dogs are the best part of the week.

Therapy Dogs and You

If you meet a therapy dog, say hello! If you want to pet him or give him a treat, ask his partner. You can ask if the dog knows any good tricks. Listen to his partner. She might know some things you can do to become fast friends with her dog. The dog might need to leave before you are ready. If it's hard to say goodbye, find out when he will be back. Saying goodbye is easier when you know you'll see your new friend again.

INTERESTING FACT

If you are afraid of dogs, you do not need to visit with a therapy dog. Just say you don't want a visit. If you can't leave the room, try to stay calm. Remember that these dogs are tested very carefully. They will not jump or bite. You can trust the dog to behave.

Therapy dogs bring smiles
wherever they go!

Boo, The Dog That Helped a Boy to Talk

Marc was a six-year-old with **selective mutism**. People with selective mutism don't talk. They know how to talk. They can make the right sounds, but something inside tells them not to. Marc didn't talk at all. Then he met Boo.

Boo is a thirteen-year-old therapy dog. Boo came to visit Marc's class. Lisa Edwards is Boo's partner. She told the children about Boo. She said there was something wrong with his brain. She told them Boo took a very long time to learn things. It took Boo two years to learn to sit and stay.

INTERESTING FACT
Marc wasn't the only person Boo helped. Boo helped so many people that Ms. Edwards wrote a book about him. It's called *A Dog Named Boo*.

When Marc got home from school that day, he was bursting with news. His mother could tell. She said, "Did something happen at school?" Marc whispered, "Boo!" Then Marc said, "I petted him! I brushed him! I love him!" From that day on, Marc was a talker. Today, Marc is in middle school. He talks a lot. He also has a dog of his own.

Boo helped Marc when nothing else seemed to work.

blood pressure (BLUD PRESH-ur) The amount that blood pushes on blood vessel walls. Very high blood pressure can be bad for health.

crisis response dogs (KRY-sis ree-SPONS DOGS) Dogs that go to places where bad things have happened. They help the people who lived through the crisis to feel better.

selective mutism (suh-LEK-tive MYOO-tism) A disorder caused by worry. The person knows how to talk and is able to, but something in the brain keeps them from talking.

therapy (THAYR-uh-pee) Things people do to help a hurt body or mind to get better.

LEARN MORE

IN THE LIBRARY

Calmenson, Stephanie. *Rosie: A Visiting Dog's Story*.
Boston, MA: Houghton Mifflin, 1999.

Goldman, Marcia. *Lola Goes to Work: A Nine-to-Five
Therapy Dog*. Berkeley, CA: Creston Books, 2013.

Markovics, Joyce L. *Therapy Dogs*. New
York: Bearport Publishing, 2014.

ON THE WEB

Visit our Web site for links about therapy dogs:
www.childsworld.com/links

*Note to Parents, Teachers, and Librarians: We routinely check our Web links to
make sure they're safe, active sites—so encourage your readers to check them out!*

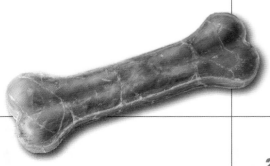

INDEX